THE FIRST EMPEROR

Written by
VICKI LOW

Illustrated by
SARA E. MAYHEW

This story is set in ancient China. Each chapter ends with a non-fiction page that gives more information about real people's lives and actual events in ancient China.

OXFORD
UNIVERSITY PRESS

PRINCE FU SU

EMPEROR ZHENG

GENERAL MENG TIAN

ZHUANG ZI

REAL PEOPLE IN HISTORY

EMPEROR ZHENG: The First Emperor of China, whose only fear is death.

PRINCE FU SU: The eldest son of Emperor Zheng and heir to the throne.

GENERAL MENG TIAN: The general in charge of building the Great Wall of China.

ZHUANG ZI: A famous wise man of ancient China.

FICTIONAL CHARACTERS

LIU: Prince Fu Su's tutor.

SIU WEN: An orphan girl who becomes a friend of the Prince.

WANG: A worker at the Great Wall who joins Prince Fu Su on his journey.

LIU

SIU WEN

WANG

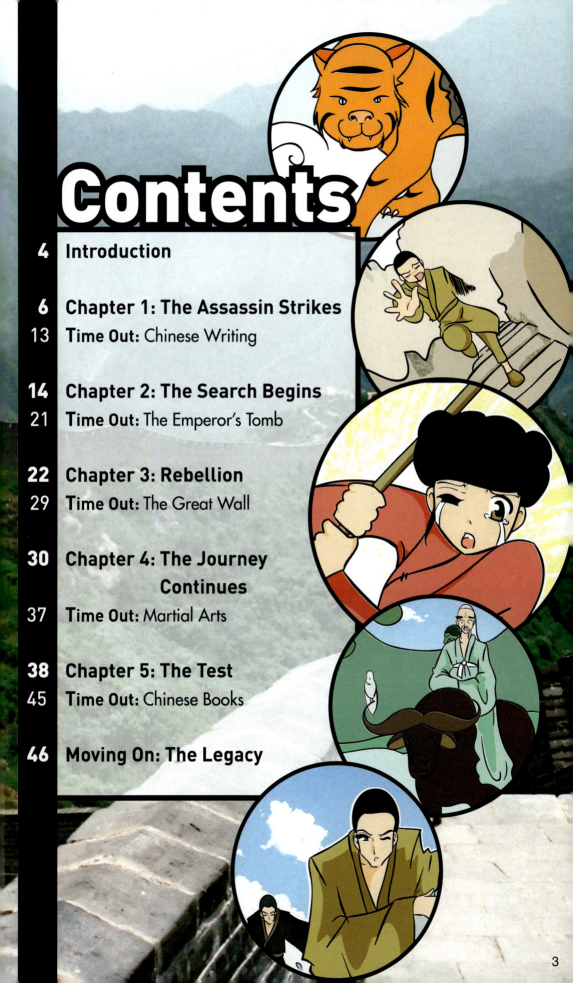

Contents

Over 2,000 years ago, China was made up of many small states that fought against one another. Then, in 221 BC/BCE, there arose a leader from the state of Qin (Chin). His name was Ying Zheng, and he unified all the warring states into one empire. Zheng called himself Shi Huang Di (also Shih Hwang-Ti), which means First Emperor.

Emperor Zheng did many great things for China. He built roads. He simplified the Chinese writing system. He made sure that everyone in China used the same money, weights and measures when they bought and sold goods. Above all, Emperor Zheng was known for building the Great Wall of China and the Tomb of the Terracotta Warriors.

Shi Huang Di

TIMELINE

The letters BCE stand for 'Before Common Era'. The years before the Common Era are counted backwards, so the greater the number, the longer ago it was. For example, 300 BCE is further in the past than 259 BCE.

300 BC/BCE >>	259 BC/BCE >>	246 BC/BCE >>	227 BC/BCE >>	221 BC/BCE >>
Qin leaders build a wall to stop attacks by invaders from the north.	Zheng, the future First Emperor of China, is born.	Zheng becomes the Qin leader at the age of 13. He begins to unify China.	An attempt is made to kill Zheng.	China is unified. Zheng becomes the First Emperor.

However, Emperor Zheng was a cruel, ruthless man. He had many enemies, and many people tried to kill him. He became very afraid of dying, and wanted more than anything to live forever.

Then Emperor Zheng heard about some magic herbs that made people live forever. In this story, Emperor Zheng sends his son, Prince Fu Su, to look for these magic herbs.

This story is set in an actual time in history, although some of the events are fictional. Real events during this period are shown on the timeline below.

219 BC/BCE >>	218 BC/BCE >>	214 BC/BCE >>	212 BC/BCE >>	210 BC/BCE >>
Emperor Zheng goes in search of the elixir of life. He wants to live forever.	Another attempt is made to kill Emperor Zheng.	General Meng Tian is put in charge of building the Great Wall.	Emperor Zheng orders the burning of books and the killing of scholars.	Emperor Zheng dies. His son Hu Hai becomes Second Emperor.

CHAPTER 1: The Assassin Strikes

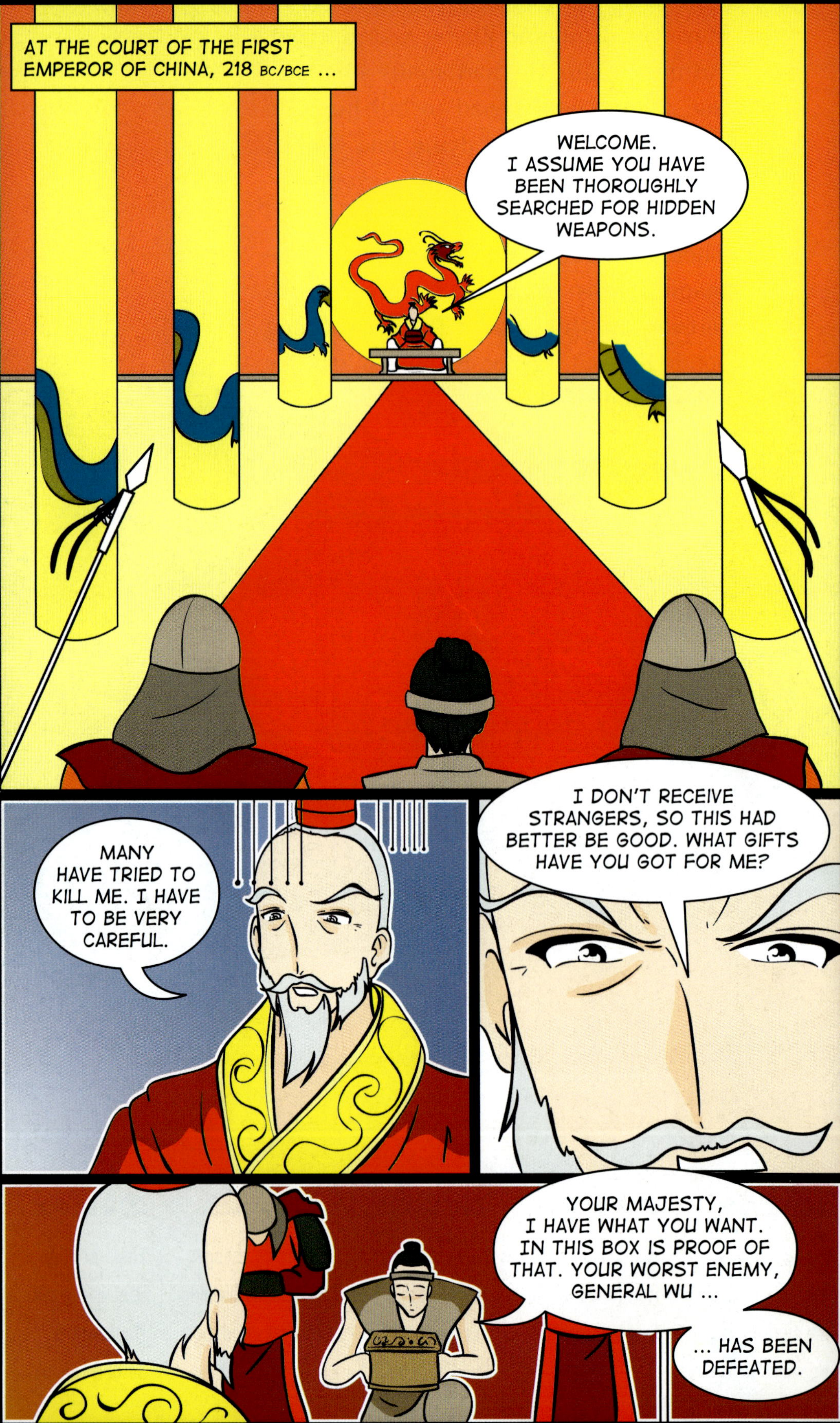

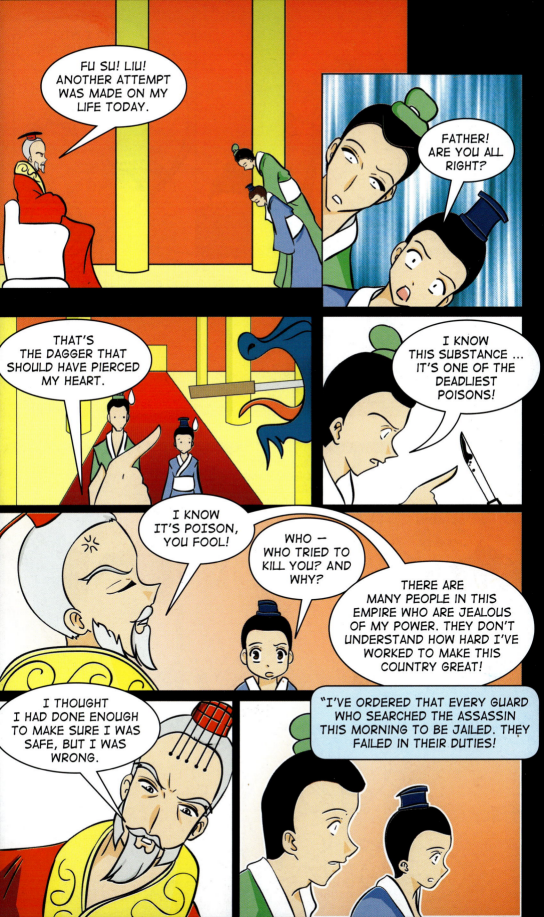

Chinese Writing

Chinese writing first appeared almost 3,500 years ago. It is one of the most beautiful but complex systems of writing ever invented. It uses symbols called characters.

The earliest form of these characters was a kind of picture writing. For example, the character for mountain, *shan*, originally looked like a drawing of three hills /\/\/\. This character now looks like this: 山. Sometimes, these 'pictures' are combined to make new words.

Today, only a small percentage of Chinese characters resemble the things they represent. Many of the characters are actually made up of two or more characters.

The Chinese have developed writing into an art form known as calligraphy. They believe that a person's calligraphy reveals much about his or her character.

female	+	child	=	good
女		子		好

field	+	strength	=	male
田		力		男

CHAPTER 2: The Search Begins

A FEW DAYS INTO THE JOURNEY ...

MY FEET HURT.

STOP COMPLAINING, YOUNG MAN.

WHY CAN'T I HAVE MY HORSE?

YOU HEARD WHAT YOUR FATHER SAID. WE HAVE TO TRAVEL LIKE PEASANTS.

BUT I'M NOT A PEASANT — I'M A PRINCE!

IF YOU WANT TO BE A GOOD EMPEROR SOME DAY, PRINCE FU SU, YOU HAVE TO KNOW HOW EVERYONE IN YOUR EMPIRE LIVES, EVEN THE POOREST PEASANT.

I DON'T THINK MY FATHER KNOWS HOW THE POOREST PEASANT LIVES.

PERHAPS HE SHOULD.

BUT WHY DO WE HAVE TO BE IN DISGUISE? WOULDN'T OUR JOURNEY BE EASIER IF EVERYONE KNEW WHO I WAS?

"LET ME EXPLAIN. YOUR FATHER BECAME THE RULER OF QIN WHEN HE WAS JUST 13, AS OLD AS YOU ARE NOW."

17

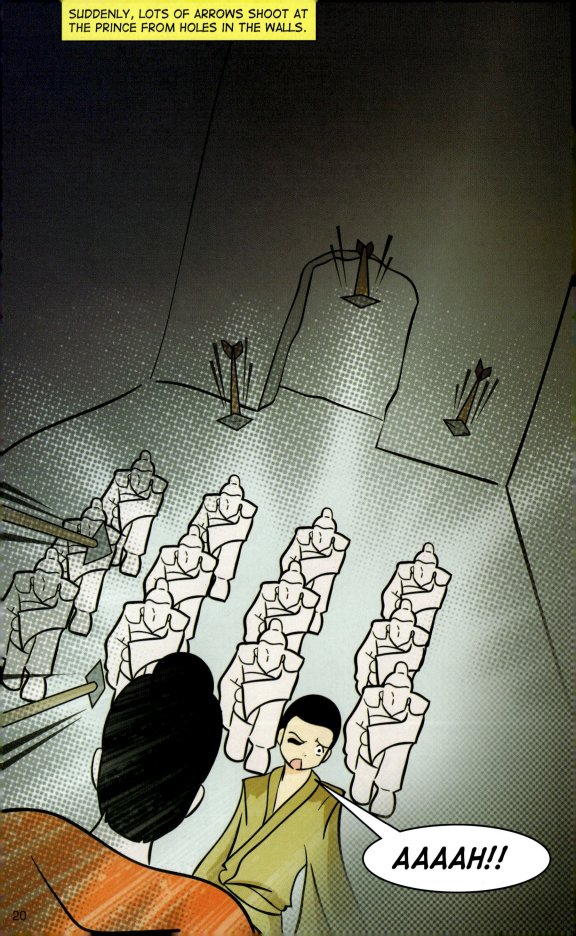

The Emperor's Tomb

*I*n 1974, a group of peasants digging a well in Xi'an in western China found some ancient objects. Archaeologists dug deeper and made an amazing discovery: thousands of life-sized terracotta (clay) warriors arranged in a military formation!

The warriors were part of the First Emperor's tomb. Emperor Zheng started to build this tomb when he became ruler at the age of 13. The tomb contains over 7,000 terracotta infantry, archers, cavalrymen and officers. Every warrior has a different face.

Buried with the warriors are real weapons – swords, daggers, spears, axes and crossbows. There are also 100 bronze chariots decorated with gold and silver. The First Emperor protected himself even after his death.

CHAPTER 3: Rebellion

27

I AM PRINCE FU SU. I'M VERY SORRY ABOUT WHAT HAPPENED TO YOUR PARENTS.

I'M LIU. WHAT'S YOUR NAME? CAN WE TAKE YOU HOME?

MY NAME IS SIU WEN. IF MY PARENTS ARE DEAD, THEN I HAVE NO HOME.

THEN COME WITH US, SIU WEN. WE'RE GOING IN SEARCH OF A WISE OLD MAN NAMED ZHUANG ZI. HE HAS MAGIC HERBS THAT CAN MAKE A PERSON LIVE FOREVER.

ALL RIGHT. I'VE NOWHERE ELSE TO GO.

GOOD!

WELCOME TO THE TEAM, SIU WEN. BUT PLEASE UNDERSTAND THAT THE MOST DANGEROUS PART OF OUR JOURNEY IS ABOUT TO BEGIN.

LIU, FU SU AND SIU WEN ARE BEING WATCHED AND FOLLOWED.

The Great Wall

*B*efore Emperor Zheng came to power, there were several walls built along the northern border of China to keep out invaders. Emperor Zheng decided to join up these walls and extend them to make a Great Wall.

The Emperor put General Meng Tian in charge of building the Great Wall. He provided soldiers, and forced peasants, prisoners and ordinary people to work on the Wall. Many died in the harsh conditions. The Great Wall has been called 'the longest graveyard in the world'.

The Wall was rebuilt during the Ming Dynasty (AD/CE 1368–1644). It has been a symbol of China for over 2,000 years. The Great Wall stretches for 6,400 km, is up to 9 m thick and 7.5 m high.

Shi Huang Di mapping the Great Wall in sand

IN THE MOUNTAINS NORTH OF THE GREAT WALL — FU SU SUSPECTS THAT THEY ARE NOT ALONE.

HMM ... I THOUGHT I HEARD SOMETHING.

STOP RIGHT THERE!

HE HAS BEEN FOLLOWING US EVER SINCE WE LEFT THE GREAT WALL.

WHO ARE YOU?

PLEASE, SIR, DON'T HURT ME. I WAS FORCED TO WORK ON THE WALL. WHEN THE FIGHTING BEGAN, I SAW MY CHANCE TO ESCAPE.

BUT WHY DIDN'T YOU JUST GO HOME?

I — I HEARD THAT YOU WERE LOOKING FOR ZHUANG ZI. I CAN HELP YOU FIND HIM.

WHAT DO YOU KNOW ABOUT US?

NOTHING! I KNOW NOTHING ABOUT YOU. PLEASE, I DON'T MEAN ANY HARM.

AAHHH!

BUT THE OLD MAN IS MORE POWERFUL THAN FU SU EXPECTS.

PLEASE, SIR. TELL ME HOW TO FIND THE ELIXIR OF LIFE. I PROMISED MY FATHER I WOULD BRING IT BACK TO HIM.

I HAVE THE MAGIC HERBS YOU ARE LOOKING FOR. BUT THERE'S MORE TO IT THAN YOU THINK.

WHAT IS IT, SIR? PLEASE TELL ME.

TO LIVE FOREVER, YOU MUST HAVE A PURE HEART OF ENDLESS LOVE FOR YOUR FELLOW BEINGS.

IF YOU TAKE THE MAGIC HERBS WITHOUT A PURE HEART, THEY WILL KILL YOU INSTEAD.

IS YOUR FATHER READY TO TAKE THE HERBS?

Martial Arts

Chinese martial arts were originally created for self-defence. Today, martial arts such as kung fu and tai chi are very popular forms of exercise all over the world. They are practised for health and physical fitness.

Kung fu is the most famous Chinese martial art. Developed by the legendary monks of the Shaolin Temple, kung fu uses the movements of animals such as the eagle, the monkey and the praying mantis.

Tai chi means supreme energy. It started as a deadly martial art. Today, it is an exercise for health and relaxation. Its slow and graceful movements are beautiful to watch, especially when they are done by hundreds of people together!

PRINCE FU SU AND HIS COMPANIONS TRAVEL BACK TO THE EMPEROR'S CAPITAL. IT TAKES THEM MANY MONTHS.

FU SU KEEPS THE MAGIC HERBS SAFE. HE DOES NOT TRUST WANG.

ONE DAY ...

DO YOU THINK MY FATHER HAS A HEART PURE ENOUGH TO TAKE THESE HERBS?

IF YOUR FATHER REALLY WANTS TO LIVE FOREVER, HE HAS TO TAKE THE RISK.

I'M WORRIED. THESE HERBS MAY KILL MY FATHER.

YOU'RE A VERY GOOD SON, FU SU. YOU HAVE DONE YOUR PART. THE REST IS UP TO HIM.

I ALSO HAVE DOUBTS ABOUT WANG. I STILL DON'T TRUST HIM.

WE'LL HAVE TO WATCH HIM CLOSELY.

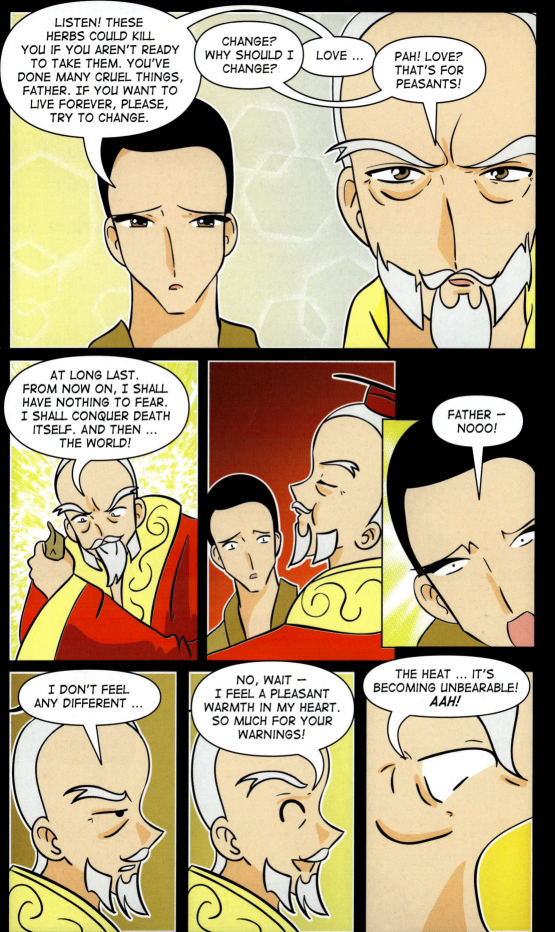

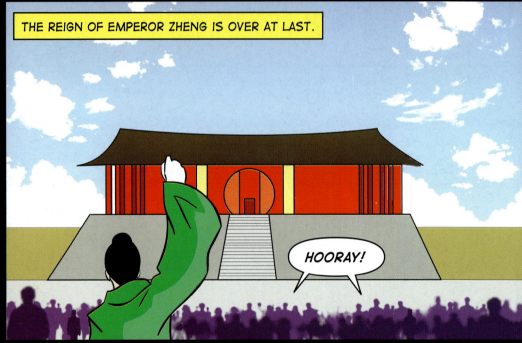

Chinese Books

*T*he First Emperor ordered the burning of all books so he could control the knowledge of his people. He spared the books that had been written with his approval, or that were about medicine and agriculture.

Paper was invented by the Chinese in AD/CE 105

Books in those days were made of long, narrow bamboo strips. These strips were tied together with silk or linen. Of course, this meant that books were very heavy. It is said that Emperor Zheng had to read through 60 kg worth of documents every day!

Chinese ink stone and ink stick

Chinese writing brushes

The Legacy

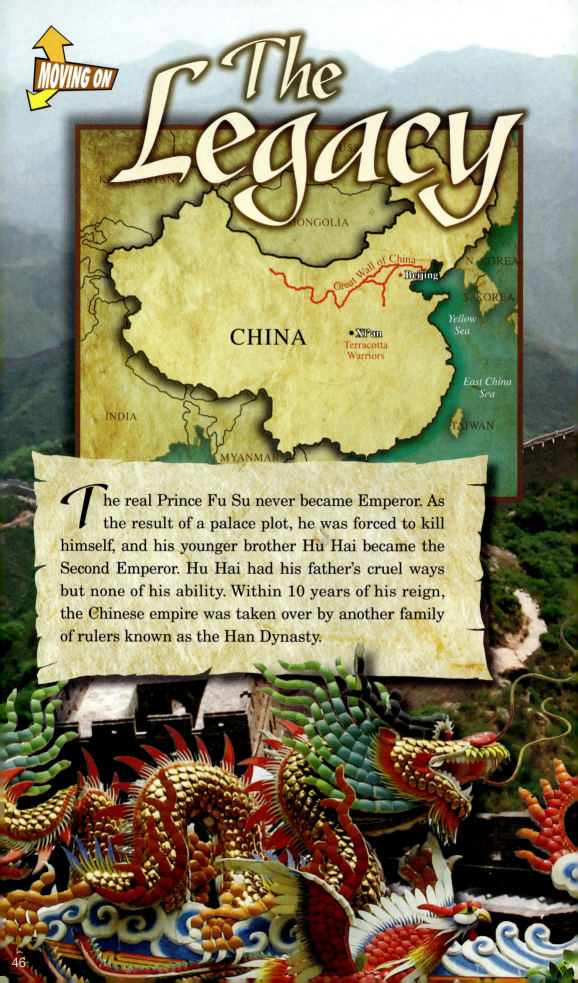

The real Prince Fu Su never became Emperor. As the result of a palace plot, he was forced to kill himself, and his younger brother Hu Hai became the Second Emperor. Hu Hai had his father's cruel ways but none of his ability. Within 10 years of his reign, the Chinese empire was taken over by another family of rulers known as the Han Dynasty.

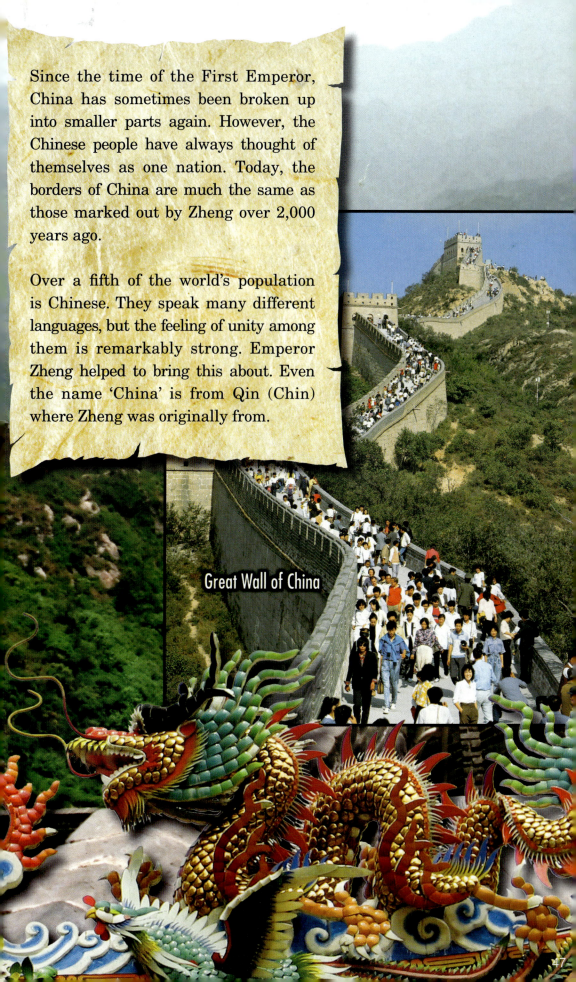

Since the time of the First Emperor, China has sometimes been broken up into smaller parts again. However, the Chinese people have always thought of themselves as one nation. Today, the borders of China are much the same as those marked out by Zheng over 2,000 years ago.

Over a fifth of the world's population is Chinese. They speak many different languages, but the feeling of unity among them is remarkably strong. Emperor Zheng helped to bring this about. Even the name 'China' is from Qin (Chin) where Zheng was originally from.

Great Wall of China

INDEX

GLOSSARY

assassin – someone who kills, or tries to kill, a person with authority and power

bandit – an outlaw such as a robber, murderer or member of a gang

barbarians – uncivilized people or community

dynasty – a line of related rulers, like kings and queens from the same family

elixir of life – a mixture that is supposed to make you live forever

legacy – something handed down by an older family member

martial arts – self-defence and fighting sports such as judo, karate, kung fu and tai chi

immortal – to live forever

imperial – belonging to an empire or its emperor

rebellion – to fight against somebody with authority and power

terracotta – a type of pottery made from baked clay

unified – to bring something together as one unit

vast – huge, immense